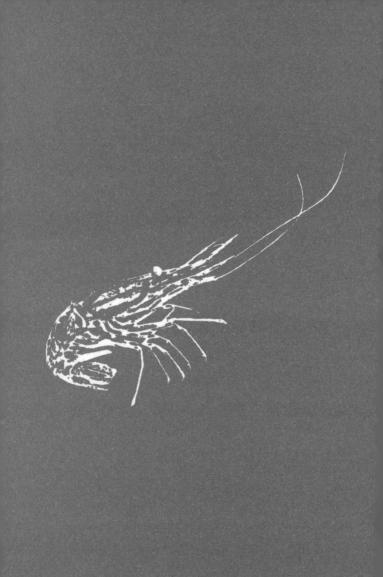

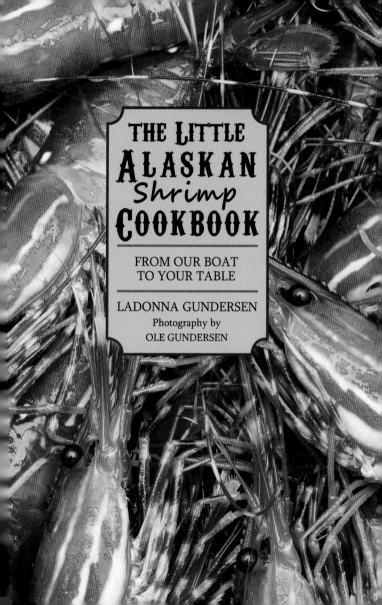

THE LITTLE
ALASKAN
Shrimp
COOKBOOK

FROM OUR BOAT
TO YOUR TABLE

LADONNA GUNDERSEN

Photography by
OLE GUNDERSEN

Published by
LaDonna Rose Publishing
Book and cover design
by Ole and LaDonna Gundersen
www.ladonnarose.com
www.facebook.com/ladonnarosecooks

Prepress and technical assistance
by S. Elyard, Todd Communications

First printing April, 2023
ISBN: 9781578338283

Distributed by
Todd Communications
611 E. 12th Ave., Suite 102
Anchorage, Alaska 99501-4603
(907) 274-TODD (8633)
Fax (907) 929-5550
With other offices in:
Juneau and Fairbanks, Alaska
sales@toddcom.com
www.alaskabooksandcalendars.com

Printed in China through **Alaska Print Brokers**,
Anchorage, Alaska.

CONTENTS

SUNDOWNER

Let's Get Started!

Fast. **Easy. Flavorful. The requirements for mouth-watering, crowd-pleasing food. You don't want to spend an hour at the stove, but you're not willing to sacrifice big, bold taste for convenience. What's the solution? Light the coals and bring on the shrimp.**

Shrimp cooks in minutes, requires minimal preparation and is the perfect foil for a wide range of seasonings, from sweet to spicy. Steeping it in marinades ensures deep flavors. Steamed, boiled or sautéed makes the perfect addition to your favorite pasta dish, skewering it makes it a fun presentation and cooking shrimp on the grill adds smoky notes that define warm-weather cooking. Not only do these meals look impressive, but they cook quickly, so dinner is on the table in a flash.

"Shrimp are as elegant as they are easy."

With drinks and appetizers on the deck, or serve these for the main course at a dinner party. Whether you dine al fresco under the stars or indoors by candlelight, putting shrimp in the limelight brings delicious rewards.

That's what this cookbook is made of. We have a collection of more than 37 recipes that will whet your appetite.

Inside, you'll find simple dishes for quick lunches, intriguing recipes for serving guests and flavorful main courses for satisfying meals.

Most recipes serve four, but many of them can be easily doubled. Though this book is mini, it will satisfy and introduce you to the world of Alaskan cuisine.

Whether it's Angel Hair Pasta with Shrimp, Rainbow Spring Roll Bowls or Shrimp Ceviche, these treasured dishes are sure to be loved by all.

The promise I try to keep with all my recipes is simple — no fancy equipment or hard to find ingredients and I take pride in the fact that anyone can make them, whether you're a five star chef or a first timer - all are a delicious addition to a cook's repertoire of recipes.

For me, cooking has always been about creating memories at the table. I hope that after I've cooked a meal for people, they remember it, tell someone about it and it becomes part of their lives – to become a part of somebody's life through food is a pretty big gift.

I hope you enjoy, devour and love this book.
I sure did enjoy making it for you.

– LaDonna Rose

SPOT SHRIMP

NORTHERN SHRIMP

COONSTRIPE SHRIMP

SIDESTRIPE SHRIMP

THE STARS
OF THE SHOW
WILD ALASKA SHRIMP

PHYSICAL DESCRIPTION
There are four major species of wild shrimp that are harvested in Alaska. Spot, (northern pink), coonstripe and sidestripe shrimp (Pandalus platyceros) are the most abundant and valuable commercial species. Shrimp in Alaska can grow to be 23 cm. in length and can live anywhere from 4-11 years.

REPRODUCTION
Most shrimp are protandric hermaphroditic and begin life as males, but then transform to females. A shrimp female can carry between 200-4,000 eggs. Eggs are found on females from October to March.

HARVEST
Harvest of shrimp in Alaska is done predominately in Southeast Alaska and to a lesser extent in Prince William Sound.

–Courtesy of
Alaska
Seafood.org

S hrimp is unquestionably the most popular seafood in America! We consume about a billion pounds of it per year. Even folks who don't like fish love shrimp and are routinely praised as the sweetest and most versatile of all seafood.

To protect the quality of the shrimp and because shrimp is shipped all over the world, commercial boat handlers flash freeze it immediately upon catching. This shellfish is available year round at most grocers and is quick and easy to cook. Because it keeps frozen for months at a time, it's a convenient ingredient to stock in your freezer for dinner in a flash. You may buy frozen shrimp for these recipes but be careful not to purchase frozen cooked shrimp. Instead, look for frozen raw shrimp.

Shrimp is marketed by size (count per pound), so pick a size that suits the meal you've planned and the number of people you're serving.

For these recipes, we call for medium shrimp–26 to 30 per pound, large shrimp–21 to 25 per pound and jumbo shrimp–16 to 20 per pound. If you can't find these sizes, buy the largest ones available. The larger the shrimp, the easier they are to peel, devein and skewer.

9

HEALTH BENEFITS OF WILD ALASKA SHRIMP

Make these protein-packed crustaceans the stars of your eat-well strategy. They're heathier than you think!

Protein helps rev up your calorie and fat- burning ability and shrimp is a stand out source: Eat 10-12 medium-size shrimp and you'll get 24g. protein (and just 99 calories and less than 1g. fat). This seafood is also high in zinc, a mineral that helps your body produce the appetite-controlling hormone leptin and iodine, which helps your thyroid function at its best, keeping your metabolism stoked.

Mood Booster and More! Shrimp serves up tryptophan, which is thought to trigger the release of the spirit-lifting hormone serotonin and vitamin B12, an antioxidant that keeps your mind sharp and alert. These little swimmers also give you a healthy dose of selenium, a mineral linked to better brain function, a strong immune system and cancer prevention.

Coming Clean on Cholesterol. Over the years, shrimp have gotten heat for being high in cholesterol. But experts believe the positives outweigh the negatives; shrimp contains almost no saturated fat and is high in heart-healthy omega-3 fatty acids and sterols - both of which are thought to bring cholesterol and triglyceride levels down as well as reduce inflammation.

Source Smart. Because it tends to be low in mercury, shrimp is a great seafood choice. However, some farmed varieties might contain antibiotics and chemicals. Your ideal pick is cold-water shrimp that's wild caught; check the Seafood Watch at montereybayaquarium.org for specific recommendations.

LET'S DO LUNCH

GINGER-SHRIMP RICE BOWL

Serves **4**

3 tablespoons **olive oil,** divided
2 **green onions,** minced, divided
3 teaspoons **garlic,** minced, divided
3 teaspoons **ginger root,** grated, divided
2 tablespoons **cranberries**
¼ cup **cashews** or shelled pistachios, roughly chopped
1 cup **wild rice blend**
2 cups organic **chicken broth**
1 pound **large shrimp,** peeled and deveined, with or without tails attached
½ teaspoon sea **salt** and ¼ teaspoon ground black **pepper**
1 head **bok choy,** chopped
2 tablespoons low-sodium **soy sauce**
1 teaspoon **rice vinegar**
¼ cup **water**
1 **avocado,** sliced or cubed
1 cup cherry **tomatoes,** halved
crumbled **feta cheese**
sliced **green onions** for garnish

In a small saucepan with a tight fitting lid, heat 1 tablespoon oil, 1 minced green onion, 1 teaspoon garlic and 1 teaspoon ginger over medium heat until fragrant. Add cranberries, nuts and rice to the pan. Cook and stir for another minute. Add broth and bring to a boil. Cover with the lid, reduce heat to low and simmer undisturbed for about 50 minutes. Remove pan from the heat.

While the rice is resting, pat the shrimp dry with paper towels and season with salt and pepper. In a large skillet, heat the remaining 2 tablespoons oil over medium-high heat. Add remaining green onions, garlic and ginger; cook until fragrant. Add the shrimp and cook for 1-2 minutes per side until just opaque and cooked through, turning them with tongs. Add the chopped bok choy. When the bok choy is bright in color, add the soy sauce, vinegar and water. Stir until the sauce is hot, about 1 minute.

To serve, divide the rice evenly among each dish. Arrange all the ingredients and garnish with more green onions and feta cheese, if desired.

SPICY SHRIMP—COCONUT NOODLE SOUP

Serves **4**

2 tablespoons **olive oil**
½ cup **onion,** chopped
1 cup button **mushrooms,** thinly sliced
1 medium **red bell pepper,** cut into strips
1 tablespoon **garlic,** minced
2 tablespoons **fresh ginger,** grated
2 tablespoons **curry paste**
6 cups organic **chicken broth**
2 tablespoons organic **fish sauce** (or soy sauce)
1 (15.5-ounce) can organic unsweetened **coconut milk**
2 tablespoons light **brown sugar**
½ teaspoon **crushed red pepper**
1 pound **large shrimp,** peeled and deveined
4 ounces **rice noodles,** broken
¼ cup **cilantro,** chopped
3 tablespoons **lime juice**
green onion strips and **lime wedges,** for garnish

Heat the oil in a large soup pot over medium heat.

Add the onion and mushrooms and sauté for 2 minutes. Add red
bell pepper, garlic and ginger and sauté until fragrant. Stir in curry
paste. Stir in chicken broth, fish sauce, coconut milk, brown sugar
and crushed red pepper. Bring to a simmer.

Stir in the shrimp and noodles, reduce heat. Simmer uncovered,
2-4 minutes or until shrimp are pink and noodles are tender. Stir
in cilantro and lime juice. If desired, top servings with green onion
strips and serve with lime wedges.

SHRIMP & SAUSAGE CORN CHILI

Serves **4**

1 pound **smoked sausage,** cut into slices
3 cups **sweet potatoes,** peeled and cut into 1-inch cubes
1 small **onion,** chopped
1 tablespoon **garlic,** minced
1 teaspoon **chili powder**
2 (15-ounce) cans **pinto beans,** rinsed and drained
1 (32-ounce) carton organic **chicken broth**
2 cups **water**
1 (15-ounce) can kernel **corn,** drained
1 **jalapeño** seeded and chopped
1 teaspoon, dried **thyme**
1 pound **medium shrimp,** peeled and deveined
fresh **parsley,** chopped

In a large soup pot over medium-high heat, add the sliced sausage
and cook until brown on each side. Remove the sausage and
reduce heat to medium.

Add the sweet potatoes, onion and garlic. Cook 4-5 minutes
or until potatoes start to brown, stirring occasionally. Stir in chili
powder, beans, broth, water, corn, jalapeño and thyme. Bring to a
boil, reduce heat to medium-low. Simmer, uncovered, 45 minutes,
stirring occasionally.

Add the sausage and shrimp. Simmer for 5 minutes and taste for
seasonings. Add salt and pepper to taste, if desired. Ladle into
warmed bowls and garnish with parsley.

SHRIMP CEASAR SALAD

Serves **4**

Croutons

4 (½-inch) thick slices **French bread**, crust removed and cut into ¾-inch cubes
1 tablespoon **olive oil**
2 tablespoons **butter,** melted
3 tablespoons **Parmesan cheese,** grated
2 large cloves **garlic,** minced

Shrimp

1 pound **large shrimp,** peeled and deveined
2 tablespoons **olive oil** or butter
sea **salt**
freshly ground black **pepper**

Dressing

2 large cloves **garlic**
3 **anchovy fillets**
½ teaspoon **lemon juice**
½ teaspoon **Dijon mustard**
½ teaspoon **Worcestershire sauce**
2 teaspoons **mayonnaise**
⅛ teaspoon sea **salt,** or as needed
¼ teaspoon freshly ground black **pepper**
¼ cup **olive oil**

Salad

1 large head **romaine** lettuce, washed, dried and torn into pieces
½ cup **Parmesan cheese,** grated
freshly ground black **pepper**

Croutons: Preheat your oven to 350˚F. In a large bowl; combine the olive oil and butter. Stir in Parmesan cheese and garlic. Add bread cubes and toss until coated. Spread the bread in a single layer on a shallow rimmed baking sheet and sprinkle with a little salt. Bake about 15 minutes or until croutons are golden, stirring once. Set aside.

Dressing: In a blender, combine the dressing ingredients until smooth.

Salad: In a large salad bowl, combine lettuce and croutons. Pour dressing over lettuce mixture; toss lightly to coat. Add ¼ cup of the Parmesan and toss well.

Shrimp: Pat the shrimp dry with paper towels. In a large non-stick sauté pan, heat the oil over medium-high heat. Add the shrimp and season lightly with salt. Cook for 1-2 minutes per side until just opaque and cooked through, turning them with tongs.

Divide Caesar salad among four plates and top with shrimp. Garnish with Parmesan and serve.

EASY SHRIMP & ORZO SALAD

Serves **4**

8 ounces **dry orzo**
2 cups **frozen corn**
¼ cup **olive oil**
2 **garlic** cloves, minced
1 large **shallot,** minced
2 **pepperoncini,** stemmed and chopped
1½ tablespoons **sherry** or red wine vinegar
1 **lemon,** zest finely grated and juiced
1 teaspoon dried **Italian seasoning**
¼ cup fresh **basil,** chopped
½ teaspoon sea **salt**
¼ teaspoon ground black **pepper**
4 **green onions,** thinly sliced
1 cup cherry **tomatoes,** halved
1 pound medium **"cooked" shrimp**
½ cup crumbled **feta cheese**

Cook the orzo according to package directions in salted water. During the last two minutes of cooking, add the frozen corn to the water. Drain the orzo and corn and run cool water over it until it's cooled, shaking off excess water.

In a large bowl, whisk together the olive oil, garlic, shallots, pepperoncini, vinegar, lemon juice and zest, Italian seasoning, basil, salt and pepper. Add the cooled orzo and corn, green onions and tomatoes. Toss to coat. Top the orzo mixture with the grilled shrimp and garnish with the feta. Serve immediately or cover and refrigerate until ready to serve.

Rainbow Spring Roll Bowls

Serves **4**

1¼ pounds **large shrimp,** peeled and deveined
1 tablespoon **olive oil** or butter
pinch of sea **salt**

Peanut Sauce

½ cup creamy natural **peanut butter**
2 teaspoons fresh **ginger,** minced
1 teaspoon **garlic,** minced
2 tablespoons **rice vinegar**
2 teaspoons **sesame oil**
⅓ cup low sodium **soy sauce**
2 teaspoons **chili paste**
2 tablespoons light **brown sugar** or honey
2 tablespoons **warm water**

For the Salad

4 ounces dry **rice noodles,** cook according to package directions
3 cups iceberg **lettuce,** shredded
⅓ cup fresh **cilantro** leaves, chopped
½ cup **mint** leaves, torn
⅓ cup **green onions,** thinly sliced
1 medium **carrot,** peeled and julienned
½ cup **cucumber,** seeded, halved and thinly sliced
1 small **red bell pepper,** cored and julienned
1 cup red **cabbage,** thinly sliced
1 large **avocado,** thinly sliced
1 cup bean or **alfalfa sprouts**

Peanut Sauce: Blend all the sauce ingredients together in a small blender or a food processor until smooth and creamy.

Pat the shrimp dry with paper towels. In a large nonstick sauté pan, heat the oil over medium-high heat. Add the shrimp and season lightly with salt. Cook for 1-2 minutes per side until just opaque and cooked through, turning them with tongs.

Assemble salads, dividing components between four bowls. Top with shrimp and drizzle each serving with peanut sauce and serve.

SHRIMP ZUCCHINI NOODLE BOWL

Serves **4**

4 medium size **zucchini,** peeled, trimmed and spiralized to create noodles
¼ teaspoon sea **salt,** plus additional to taste
1 **lemon,** zest finely grated and juiced
2 **garlic** cloves, minced
½ cup packed fresh **basil** leaves, roughly chopped
½ cup fresh flat-leaf **parsley,** chopped
3 tablespoons **olive oil**
fresh ground black **pepper,** to taste
1 pound **large shrimp,** peeled and deveined
1 pint multi colored cherry **tomatoes,** halved
¼ cup **Parmesan cheese,** for serving

In a medium bowl, toss noodles with ¼ teaspoon salt and transfer to a colander for about 15 minutes to drain excess water.

Meanwhile, in a large bowl, combine lemon juice and zest, garlic, basil, parsley and olive oil.

Pat the shrimp dry with paper towels. In a large nonstick sauté pan, heat 1 tablespoon oil over medium-high heat. Add the shrimp and season lightly with salt. Cook for 1-2 minutes per side until just opaque and cooked through, turning them with tongs. Remove them and keep warm.

Arrange the noodles on a large tray lined with paper towels. Pat dry to absorb any excess water. Add the noodles to bowl with herb mixture and toss gently to combine. Season with pepper and additional salt to taste. Transfer to serving bowls and top with tomatoes, shrimp and Parmesan cheese.

dance with the waves, move with the sea, let the rhythm of the water set your soul free

Spicy Shrimp Burrito Bowls

Serves **4**

Cilantro Rice

1 cup **jasmine rice,** cook according to package directions
1 tablespoon **lime juice**
1 tablespoon **sugar**
½ teaspoon sea **salt**
¼ cup fresh **cilantro,** chopped
<u>**Once the rice is done, mix in the lime juice, sugar, salt and cilantro.**</u>

Corn Salsa

1 (15-ounce) can kernel **corn,** rinsed and drained
1 (15-ounce) can **black beans,** rinsed and drained
½ cup **red onion,** diced
1 cup **tomatoes,** chopped (any type)
⅓ bunch **cilantro,** chopped
2 **garlic** cloves, minced
1 small **jalapeño,** seeded, minced
2 tablespoons **lime juice**
sea **salt,** if desired
<u>**In a medium sized bowl, mix all ingredients together.**</u>

Spicy Shrimp

¼ teaspoon **cayenne** pepper
¼ teaspoon **garlic powder**
1½ teaspoons **chili powder**
1½ teaspoons ground **cumin**
1½ pounds **medium shrimp,** peeled and deveined
1 tablespoon **olive oil**
<u>**Mix the spices together in a small bowl and set aside.**</u>

Optional toppings: fresh cilantro, sliced avocado, sour cream or tortilla strips.

Pat the shrimp dry with paper towels. Toss the shrimp in the spice seasoning. In a large nonstick sauté pan, heat 1 tablespoon oil over medium-high heat. Add the shrimp and cook for 1-2 minutes per side until just opaque and cooked through, turning them with tongs.

Divide cooked rice into four bowls. Top each bowl with ¼ of the corn salsa, avocado and shrimp. Top with any of the toppings you desire.

SHRIMP & PINEAPPLE FRIED RICE

Serves **4**

1 tablespoon **butter**
2 tablespoons **olive oil,** divided
1 ripe **pineapple,** chopped into bite-size pieces
1 tablespoon **sesame oil**
1 pound **medium shrimp,** peeled, deveined
1 medium **onion,** chopped
1 tablespoon **curry** powder
½ teaspoon **ginger** powder
6 **garlic** cloves minced
¼ teaspoon **red pepper flakes,** optional
4 cups **cooked CHILLED jasmine rice**
¼ teaspoon sea **salt** and ⅛ teaspoon ground black **pepper**
1 cup **raisins**
½ cup roasted **cashews**
1 cup cherry **tomatoes,** cut in half
3 tablespoons **organic fish sauce** (or soy sauce)
2 teaspoons **sugar**
4 **green onions,** thinly sliced

Melt butter with 1 tablespoon olive oil in a large wok or nonstick frying pan over medium heat. Increase to medium-high and add the pineapple. Cook stirring constantly, for 5 minutes or until pineapple caramelizes. Remove to a plate using a slotted spoon. Add 1 tablespoon olive oil and sesame oil to the pan. Add the shrimp and cook for 1-2 minutes per side until just opaque and cooked through, turning them with tongs. Transfer shrimp to the pineapple plate.

Add onions to the pan and cook over medium heat. Add the curry powder, ginger powder, garlic and red pepper flakes, stirring constantly. **Stir in the CHILLED rice,** salt and pepper and spread into an even layer. Let rice cook for about 2 minutes, then flip rice over and pat again and resist the urge to stir for 2 more minutes.

Add the raisins, cashews, tomatoes, pineapple and shrimp to the pan (reserving some shrimp for garnish) along with the fish sauce and sugar, stir to combine. Transfer to hollowed out pineapples or to bowls and garnish with green onions and shrimp. Serve with soy sauce, if desired.

SHRIMP ON A STICK

CITRUS-MARINATED SHRIMP

Serves **4**

¼ cup **olive oil**
1 tablespoon grated **grapefruit peel**
1 tablespoon grated **lemon peel**
1 tablespoon grated **orange peel**
1 teaspoon fresh **mint,** chopped
½ teaspoon sea **salt**
1½ pounds **large shrimp,** peeled and deveined

In a medium bowl, stir together all ingredients except shrimp. Stir in shrimp to coat; cover and refrigerate 2 hours.

Preheat an outdoor grill or stove-top grill pan to medium heat. Remove shrimp from marinade, keeping them coated with citrus peel and mint; discard remaining marinade. Thread shrimp onto 4 metal skewers.

Clean and oil the grates. Grill shrimp, flipping once, until firm and opaque throughout.

SHRIMP IN BEER MARINADE

Serves **4**

1 (12-ounce) bottle white **beer** or your favorite beer
1 tablespoon fresh **ginger,** grated
2 teaspoons **Dijon mustard**
½ teaspoon sea **salt**
¼ teaspoon ground black **pepper**
1½ pounds **large shrimp,** peeled and deveined

In a large bowl, whisk together all ingredients except shrimp. Stir in shrimp to coat. Cover and refrigerate 2 hours.

Preheat an outdoor grill or stove-top grill pan to medium heat. Thread shrimp onto 4 metal skewers.

Clean and oil the grates. Grill the shrimp, flipping once, until firm and opaque throughout, 4-6 minutes, brushing occasionally with marinade.

SPICY GRILLED SHRIMP KEBABS

Serves **4**

¼ cup **lemon juice,** divided
¼ cup **olive oil**
2 tablespoons fresh **ginger,** minced
1½ tablespoons **garlic,** minced
½ teaspoons sea **salt**
1 teaspoon **sugar**
½ teaspoon **red chili flakes**
1½ pounds **large or jumbo shrimp,** peeled and deveined, tails left on
1½ cups **cherry tomatoes**
lemon wedges

Cilantro Aioli

1½ cups **mayonnaise**
¼ cup **lemon juice**
2 tablespoons fresh **ginger,** minced
1½ tablespoons **garlic,** minced
½ teaspoon sea **salt**
¼ to ½ teaspoon **red chili flakes**
1 cup fresh **cilantro** sprigs

In a medium bowl, mix lemon juice, olive oil, ginger, garlic, salt, sugar and chili flakes. Add the shrimp and mix to coat. Cover and refrigerate about 1 hour, stirring once or twice.

Aioli: Combine mayonnaise, lemon juice, ginger, garlic, salt, chili flakes and cilantro in a food processor. Whirl until smooth. Scrape aioli into a small bowl, cover and refrigerate until ready to use.

Preheat an outdoor grill or stove-top grill pan to medium heat.

Clean and oil the grates. Thread the shrimp on to 4 metal skewers, interspersing with cherry tomatoes. Grill shrimp, flipping once, until firm and opaque throughout. Transfer kebabs to a platter; garnish with lemon wedges and cilantro sprigs. Serve with Cilantro aioli.

GREEK GRILLED SHRIMP

Makes **4**

½ cup **olive oil**
2 tablespoons **capers,** drained, coarsely chopped
2 **garlic** cloves, coarsely chopped
2 tablespoons fresh **dill,** chopped
1 tablespoon fresh **oregano,** chopped
2 teaspoons finely grated **lemon zest**
2 teaspoons **fennel seeds,** crushed
1 teaspoon sea **salt**
½ teaspoon freshly ground black **pepper**
1½ pound **large shrimp,** peeled and deveined
1 (14-ounce) can **artichoke hearts,** drained, halved
12 **cherry tomatoes**
½ cup crumbled **feta cheese**

In a large bowl, stir together oil, capers, garlic, dill, oregano, lemon zest, fennel seeds, salt and pepper. Stir in shrimp to coat; cover and refrigerate at least 2 hours or up to 4 hours.

Preheat an outdoor grill or stove-top grill pan to medium heat. Equally divide and thread shrimp, artichoke hearts and tomatoes onto skewers. Brush marinade over shrimp.

Clean and oil the grates. Grill shrimp, flipping once, until firm and opaque throughout. Place feta on shrimp. Cook until cheese is melted and serve.

A Note from LaDonna Rose
If you are using wooden skewers, make sure you soak them for 30 minutes before threading everything on to them. This will ensure that they don't burn when cooking.

KIELBASA & SHRIMP LOLLIPOPS

Makes **20**
20 (6-inch) **bamboo skewers,** soaked
20 jumbo or **extra-large shrimp,** peeled, tails left on
13.5 ounces fully cooked smoked **Kielbasa,** sliced on the bias into twenty
1/2-inch thick pieces
olive oil
freshly ground black **pepper**

Thread one shrimp and one piece of sausage onto each skewer, brush with oil and season with pepper.

Preheat an outdoor grill or stove-top grill pan to medium heat. **Clean** and oil the grates.

Grill skewers, covered, until shrimp are opaque and the sausage is lightly charred, turning once half way through.

HONEY GARLIC SHRIMP

Serves **4**
2 pounds **extra-jumbo shrimp,** peeled and deveined, tails left on
¾ teaspoon sea **salt**
freshly ground black **pepper**
1 tablespoon **olive oil**
⅓ cup **honey**
2 tablespoons **chili garlic sauce**

Whisk the honey and chili sauce together in a small bowl.

Preheat an outdoor grill or stove-top grill pan to medium heat. **Clean** and oil the grates.

Thread shrimp on to metal skewers. Use a pastry brush to coat each side of the kebabs with oil. Season with salt and pepper. Grill shrimp, flipping once and brushing with the honey mixture. Grill until firm and opaque throughout, about 2 minutes. Brush again and serve hot.

Pesto Shrimp Kebabs

Serves **4**

1 pound **medium** or **large shrimp,** peeled and deveined
⅓ cup store-bought **pesto**
2 tablespoons **butter,** melted
pinch **garlic powder**
sea **salt** and ground black **pepper**
lemon slices, for garnish (optional)

Place shrimp and pesto in a large zip-top plastic bag or bowl and mix well to coat the shrimp. Place in the refrigerator to marinate for 30 minutes, then thread the shrimp onto skewers.

Preheat an outdoor grill to medium heat. Clean and oil the grates. Grill shrimp, flipping once, until firm and opaque throughout.

Mix the melted butter and the garlic powder together in a small bowl. Drizzle each kabob with some of the melted butter. Season with salt and pepper to taste and garnish with lemon slices if desired.

Grilled Garlic Shrimp

Serves **4**

1 pound **large shrimp,** peeled and deveined
¼ cup **olive oil**
¼ cup fresh **cilantro,** finely chopped
¼ cup fresh flat leaf **parsley,** finely chopped
4-6 **garlic cloves,** minced
1 tablespoon **lemon juice**
½ teaspoon sea **salt and** ¼ teaspoon ground black **pepper**
pinch of ground **cayenne pepper**

In a medium bowl, stir together all ingredients except shrimp. Place the shrimp in a bowl and pour ¾ of the marinade on top of the shrimp. Mix gently until shrimp are well coated. Cover the bowl and marinate the shrimp for 30 minutes to an hour. **Thread the shrimp** on to 4 metal skewers and make sure to get all the good garlic and herbs from the bowl and spread on the shrimp. **Preheat an outdoor grill to medium heat. Clean and oil the grates.** Grill shrimp, flipping once, until firm and opaque throughout. Spoon the remaining marinade on top of the shrimp before serving.

GARLIC SHRIMP

Serves 4

3 tablespoons **olive oil**
1 tablespoon **butter**
12 cloves, **garlic** divided
1 pound **large shrimp,** peeled and deveined
¼ teaspoon crushed **red pepper flakes**
½ teaspoon sea **salt**
1½ teaspoons **sherry vinegar**
2 tablespoons **parsley,** chopped
crusty bread or **baguette**

In a 12-inch cast iron skillet (or other heavy frying pan), heat the oil and butter over medium-low heat.

Meanwhile, using the flat side of a chef's knife, smash 4 garlic cloves. Add the garlic to the oil. Cook, stirring occasionally, until the garlic is light golden brown, 3 to 4 minutes. Remove the pan from the heat and allow the oil to cool to room temperature. Using a slotted spoon, remove the smashed garlic from the skillet and discard.

Thinly slice the remaining 8 garlic cloves. Return the skillet to medium-low heat and add the sliced garlic and red pepper flakes. Cook, stirring occasionally, until the garlic is tender but not browned, 3 to 4 minutes. Increase heat to medium.

Pat the shrimp dry with paper towels and season with salt. Add the shrimp to the pan in a single layer. Cook the shrimp undisturbed, until the oil starts to gently bubble, about 2 minutes. Using tongs, flip the shrimp and continue to cook until almost cooked through, about 2 minutes longer. Increase the heat to medium-high and add the sherry vinegar and parsley. Cook stirring constantly, until the shrimp are cooked through. Serve immediately with crusty bread or baguette.

Roasted Shrimp with Rosemary & Thyme

Serves **4**

½ cup **olive oil**
3 large fresh **rosemary sprigs,** halved
4 fresh **thyme sprigs**
freshly ground black **pepper**
1½ pounds large **shrimp,** peeled and deveined
½ teaspoon sea **salt**

Preheat your oven to 400°F.

Pour the oil into a 9 x 13-inch rimmed baking dish. Add the rosemary, thyme, 1 teaspoon pepper and bake until the mixture is fragrant, about 10 minutes. **Add** the shrimp to the dish and toss with tongs until coated. Bake the shrimp until opaque and firm about 10 minutes. **Add** a sprinkling of salt, toss well and serve.

Fennel & Garlic Shrimp

Serves **2-3**

6 tablespoons **olive oil** (can use ½ oil ½ butter)
1 cup **fennel bulb,** chopped, fronds reserved
3 tablespoons **garlic,** minced
¼ teaspoon crushed **red pepper flakes**
1 pound jumbo **shrimp,** peeled and deveined
1 tablespoon fresh **parsley,** chopped
½ teaspoon sea **salt** and ¼ teaspoon freshly ground black **pepper**
French bread, for serving

Heat the oil in a large nonstick sauté pan over medium-high heat. Add fennel and sauté for 5 minutes, until tender but not browned. Turn heat to medium-low, add garlic and red pepper flakes. Cook at a very low sizzle for 2-3 minutes. **Pat the shrimp dry with paper towels,** add them to the pan and toss together with the fennel and oil. Spread the shrimp in one layer and cook over medium heat for 1-2 minutes per side, until they're opaque and cooked through, turning them with tongs. **Off the heat,** sprinkle with parsley, 1 tablespoon of chopped fennel fronds, salt and pepper. Serve with bread to soak up all the pan juices.

SHRIMP COCKTAIL

Serves 4

1 pound **medium or large shrimp,** peeled and deveined, tails left on
2 teaspoons sea **salt**
6 black **peppercorns**
1 **bay leaf**
1 **lemon,** juiced

Cocktail Sauce
1 cup **ketchup**
1 **lemon,** (small) zest finely grated and juiced
4 teaspoons prepared **horseradish**
¼ teaspoon **Worcestershire sauce**

In a large pot, add cold water, salt, peppercorns, bay leaf and the juice of one lemon. Bring the mixture to a boil and cook for 5 minutes. Remove the pot of boiling water from the heat and add in the shrimp. Let the shrimp sit in the pot for 2-3 minutes or until the shrimp becomes opaque and the tails begin to curl.

Meanwhile, in a large bowl, add cold water and ice. Use a slotted spoon to transfer the shrimp to the ice bath, Let the shrimp sit for 5 minutes. Drain the shrimp and place on a serving platter. Squeeze the second lemon over the shrimp. Chill the shrimp while you make the cocktail sauce.

Cocktail Sauce: Whisk together ketchup, lemon juice and zest and Worcestershire in a small bowl. Whisk in 1 teaspoon horseradish at a time until your desired taste.

Serve the shrimp immediately with cocktail sauce or store in the refrigerator until ready to serve.

SHRIMP CROSTINI

Makes **24**

1 (8-ounce) package **cream cheese,** softened
¼ cup **mayonnaise**
5 cloves **garlic,** minced and divided
1 tablespoon **green onion,** minced
pinch of sea **salt**
¼ cup **butter**
1 tablespoon fresh **parsley,** minced
1 pound **medium shrimp** peeled and deveined, tails left on or off
24 toasted **baguette** slices **Preheat your oven to 350˚F. Brush both sides with olive oil and season with sea salt. Bake until golden.**

Garnish: halved cherry **tomatoes,** fresh flat leaf **parsley** leaves

In a small bowl, combine cream cheese, mayonnaise, 2 garlic cloves and green onions; set aside.

In a large skillet, melt butter over medium heat. Add remaining 3 cloves garlic and parsley; cook for 3 minutes. Add shrimp; cook for 3-4 minutes or until pink and firm.

Spread cream cheese mixture evenly over bread rounds. Top each with 1 shrimp. Garnish with tomato halves and parsley leaves.

A Note from LaDonna Rose
Instead of standing the shrimp up, take the tails off and lay them on their sides. It makes them a little easier to eat. Adding a small amount of avocado is extra yummy.

COCONUT SHRIMP

Serves 4

Green Goddess Dip

½ cup **mayonnaise**
½ cup **sour cream**
¼ cup low-fat **buttermilk**
3 tablespoons **white vinegar**
1 teaspoon **anchovy paste** (or 1-2 anchovy fillets)
2 **garlic** cloves
1 teaspoon Dijon **mustard**
2 tablespoons fresh **basil** leaves
2 tablespoons fresh **dill**
2 tablespoons Italian **parsley**
2 tablespoons fresh **mint** leaves
sea **salt** and freshly ground black **pepper**

Shrimp

1 pound **medium shrimp,** peeled and deveined, tails left on
½ teaspoon sea **salt**
2 cups flaked **coconut**
3 tablespoons all-purpose **flour**
2-3 **egg whites,** whisked
olive oil, for frying

Dipping Sauce: Combine all ingredients except salt and pepper in a blender until smooth. Season with salt and pepper. Cover and refrigerate until smooth.

Shrimp: Pat the shrimp dry with paper towels and season with salt. On a large plate, mix together coconut and flour. Dip each shrimp into egg whites, then roll in the coconut mixture.

In a large skillet over medium-high heat, add about ¼ inch oil. When oil is sizzling, carefully add 3-4 shrimp at a time and cook until coconut is golden brown, about 2 minutes per side. Remove shrimp with a slotted spoon and transfer to a paper-towel lined plate. Serve with the dipping sauce.

SIMPLE SHRIMP SCAMPI

2 tablespoons **olive oil**
4 tablespoons **butter, divided**
1½ tablespoons **garlic,** minced
1½ pounds **medium or large shrimp,** peeled and deveined, tails left on
sea **salt** and fresh ground black **pepper** to taste
¼ cup **white wine** or organic chicken broth
⅛ teaspoon **crushed red pepper**
2 tablespoons **lemon juice**
¼ cup fresh **parsley,** chopped

Heat the olive oil and 2 tablespoons of butter in a large skillet. Add garlic and sauté about 30 seconds. Add the shrimp and sauté for 1-2 minutes on one side, then flip.

Pour in wine (or broth), add red pepper flakes. Bring to a slow simmer for 2 minutes and the shrimp is cooked through. Stir in remaining butter, lemon juice and parsley.

A Note from LaDonna Rose

Although this dish goes very well with rice or noodles, it is really at its best with garlic bread. Make it in a skillet and bring the pan to the table; serve the shrimp with a spoon and use the bread to sop up remaining juices from both plate and skillet— there are few greater pleasures.

SHRIMP & BANANA CEVICHE

Serves 2-4

16 medium **"cooked" shrimp,** peeled and deveined
1 medium **"firm" avocado,** pitted, peeled, cut into small thin slices
2 small **"firm" bananas,** thinly sliced
½ cup **red onion,** cut into small thin slices
2 tablespoons fresh **lime juice**
2 tablespoons fresh **orange juice**
2 tablespoons **olive oil**
¼ cup fresh **cilantro,** chopped
1 small **serrano chili,** thinly sliced
pinch **red pepper flakes**

Fold the shrimp, avocado, bananas and red onion in a bowl. Add lime juice, orange juice, olive oil, cilantro, serrano chili and a pinch of red pepper flakes. Serve.

SHRIMP SALSA

Makes 2 cups

½ cup **tomatoes,** seeded, diced
½ cup **red radishes,** minced
¼ cup **red onion,** minced
¼ cup fresh **cilantro,** minced
1 teaspoon **garlic,** minced
8 medium or large **shrimp,** peeled and deveined
1 teaspoon **olive oil**
¼ teaspoon sea **salt**
⅛ teaspoon ground black **pepper**
2 tablespoons fresh **lime juice**
6 shots of **Tabasco sauce**

Preheat an outdoor grill or stove-top grill pan to medium heat.

Combine tomatoes, radishes, onion, cilantro and garlic in a bowl.

Toss shrimp with oil, salt and pepper. Grill shrimp until cooked through, about 2 minutes per side. Remove from grill. When cool enough to handle, chop into bite-sized pieces and add to tomato mixture. Stir in lime juice and Tabasco. Serve with bruschetta of choice.

SOFT SPRING ROLLS WITH SHRIMP

Makes 6

6 ounces thin **dried rice noodles,** cook according to package directions
10 **"cooked" medium shrimp,** peeled and cut in half lengthwise
6 round **rice paper sheets**
6 **boston lettuce leaves,** thick stem ends removed, cut in half
1 cup **carrots,** shredded
1 cup **red cabbage,** thinly shredded
6 **green onions,** cut in 3-inch lengths and sliced lengthwise into thin strips
24 fresh **mint leaves**
½ cup **cilantro** leaves, lightly packed
Peanut Sauce, page 22

Arrange all the ingredients separately around a large cutting board or tray set before you. Set out a platter to hold the finished rolls, as well as a large shallow bowl filled with cool water, large enough to hold the piece of rice paper. Set a clean damp dish towel on the cutting board.

To make each roll, slide one sheet of rice paper into the pan of cool water and press gently to submerge it for about 10 seconds. Remove it carefully, draining the water and place it before you on the damp cloth.

Lay one piece of lettuce over the bottom third of the rice paper. On the lettuce, place 2-3 tablespoons of noodles, 1 tablespoon carrots, 1 tablespoon of cabbage and a few green onions. Roll the paper halfway into a cylinder. Fold the sides in a envelope pattern.

Lay 3 shrimp halves, cut side up, along the crease. Place a few cilantro and mint leaves next to the shrimp. Roll the paper into a tight cylinder to seal. Repeat with remaining wrappers. Serve immediately with the peanut dipping sauce, if desired.

SHRIMP TACOS WITH AVOCADO-MANGO SALSA

Serves 4

1 medium **mango,** diced
1 medium **avocado,** diced
½ cup **red onion,** diced
¼ cup fresh **cilantro,** chopped
2 tablespoons **lime juice**
1 pound **medium shrimp,** peeled, deveined and halved lengthwise
1 teaspoon **chili powder**
¼ teaspoon sea **salt**
2 tablespoons **butter**
8 (6-inch) corn or flour **tortillas,** warmed according to package directions

Combine mango, avocado, onion, cilantro and lime juice in a bowl; set aside.

Pat shrimp dry with paper towels and season with chili powder and salt. In a large nonstick skillet, heat the butter over medium-high heat. Add the shrimp and cook for 1-2 minutes per side until just opaque and cooked through, turning them with tongs.

Spoon shrimp into tortillas; top with salsa. Serve with lime wedges.

Courtesy of Alaska Seafood.org

SHRIMP & BACON QUESADILLAS

Makes 2

4 **bacon** slices, chopped
½ pound **medium shrimp,** peeled, deveined and halved lengthwise
2 teaspoons **olive oil,** divided
2 (10-inch) **flour tortillas**
1 **vine tomato,** seeded and diced
1 small **avocado,** diced
¼ cup **green onions,** chopped
¼ cup **cilantro,** finely chopped
1½ cups shredded **jack cheese**

Cook the bacon in a medium frying pan over medium-high heat until crisp. Transfer to a paper towel to drain. Pour off grease, then add shrimp to the pan and cook until pink, about 1 minute, stirring often. Set aside and carefully wipe out the pan.

Heat 1 teaspoon oil in a large frying pan over medium heat. Set tortilla in pan and sprinkle half of it with bacon, shrimp, tomatoes, avocado, green onions, cilantro and cheese. Fold tortilla over filling and press down gently. Cook, covered, until brown, turning once, about 3 minutes total. Transfer to a plate. Repeat to make the second quesadilla. Cut into wedges and serve with salsa and sour cream.

MAIN DISHES

SHRIMP CAKE SANDWICHES

Makes **8 cakes**

1 pound **medium shrimp,** peeled, deveined and roughly chopped
2 cups panko **bread crumbs,** plus 1 cup for forming
3 **green onions,** minced
2 tablespoons fresh **parsley,** minced
2 tablespoons fresh **chives,** minced
4 **eggs**
1 tablespoon **lemon juice**
1 teaspoon **Dijon mustard**
1 teaspoon **Worcestershire sauce**
½ teaspoon sea **salt**
½ teaspoon ground **cayenne**

<u>Fry In</u>
olive oil

<u>Serve With</u>

<u>Rémoulade Sauce</u>
¾ cup **mayonnaise**
1½ tablespoons **Dijon mustard**
2 teaspoons **lemon juice**
2 teaspoons **Worcestershire sauce**
½ teaspoon **smoked paprika**
1½ teaspoons **hot sauce**
1½ tablespoons **sweet relish**
pinch of sea **salt**
black **pepper** to taste

Mix together all ingredients in a small bowl. Serve immediately or refrigerate.

toasted bread, lettuce, cooked bacon strips, sliced avocado and Rémoulade Sauce

In a large bowl, combine shrimp, 2 cups bread crumbs, green onions, parsley, chives, eggs, lemon juice, mustard, Worcestershire sauce, salt and cayenne.

Dividing evenly, form mixture into 8 cakes. Dredge each mound in bread crumbs to coat and chill for one hour.

In a large nonstick skillet over medium-high heat; sauté half of the cakes in 1½ tablespoons of oil. Cook until golden, about 3 minutes, then carefully flip the cakes over and cook on the other side about 3 minutes more. Transfer to a paper-towel-lined plate. Sauté remaining cakes in the same manner.

Serve on toast with lettuce, bacon, avocado and Rémoulade sauce.

SHRIMP BURGERS WITH BASIL AIOLI

Makes **4**

1 pound **medium shrimp,** peeled and deveined
1 **egg**
1 **shallot**, minced
1 tablespoon **garlic,** minced
½ **jalapeño,** seeded and minced
2 tablespoons fresh **cilantro,** minced
½ cup panko **bread crumbs**
⅓ cup **red bell pepper,** minced
½ teaspoon sea **salt** and ¼ teaspoon ground black **pepper**
1 teaspoon finely grated **lemon zest**
2 tablespoons **olive oil**

<u>Basil Pesto Aioli</u>
¼ cup purchased or homemade **basil pesto**
¼ cup **mayonnaise**
In a small bowl, combine pesto and mayonnaise and mix well.

4 **brioche buns**
lettuce leaves
4 **tomato slices**

Divide the shrimp in half. Coarsely chop one half and set aside.
Put remaining half in a food processor and grind to a coarse puree.
Add egg, shallot, garlic, jalapeño, and cilantro. Process until
smooth. Sprinkle mixture with bread crumbs and pulse again.
Transfer contents of food processor to a large bowl. Add coarsely
chopped shrimp, red bell pepper, salt, pepper and lemon zest.
Divide into 4 patties and chill for one hour.

Heat the oil in a large frying pan over medium-high heat. Cook
the patties for 3-4 minutes per side, until golden in color. To keep
the patties from falling apart when cooking, make sure the pan
is hot before adding them, allow them to cook for 3-4 minutes
without touching so that a golden crust forms before flipping over.
Place patties on a paper towel to drain. **To prepare your burgers,**
lightly toast the buns and spread the pesto on each. Add some
lettuce, a slice of tomato and your shrimp patty and enjoy.

GRILLED SHRIMP REUBEN

Makes **4**

<u>**Thousand Island Dressing**</u>

½ cup **mayonnaise**
1 tablespoon **sweet relish,** drained
1 tablespoon **ketchup**
Stir all in a small bowl until well blended.

8 slices Russian **rye bread**
8 slices **Swiss cheese,** more if needed
2 cups **"cooked" small or medium shrimp,** cut into bite-sized pieces
2 cups **sauerkraut,** drained
¼ cup **butter,** softened, more if needed
4 slices **dill pickle**

Arrange the bread slices on a work surface and spread a little of the dressing on each slice. Put a slice of cheese on each piece of bread; divide the shrimp among 4 of the slices, then top each with sauerkraut.

Invert the remaining cheese-covered bread slices onto each sandwich and spread butter on top of each. Melt the remaining butter in a large nonstick skillet over medium heat. Arrange the sandwiches, butter-side up in the pan and grill each side until toasty and cheese is melted. Top with a sliced pickle.

SHRIMP PITA PIZZA

Makes **2**

2 (7-8-inch) **pita bread** (naan or ready-made thin pizza crust)
½ cup canned **tomato sauce**
2 teaspoons **garlic,** minced
2 teaspoons **chili garlic sauce**
½ pound **medium shrimp,** shelled and deveined, split in half lengthwise
1 cup **Gruyère cheese,** shredded
½ cup aged or fresh **goat cheese,** crumbled
¼ cup fresh **cilantro,** chopped
¼ cup fresh **basil,** chopped
2 teaspoons finely grated **lime zest**

Preheat your oven to 350°F. Lay the pita bread on a sheet pan covered with parchment paper.

In a small bowl, combine the tomato sauce, garlic and chili sauce. Spread the sauce on each pita bread. Place the shrimp on top and top with the cheese.

Bake for 15 minutes or until cheese is melted and bubbly.

Remove the pizza from the oven and sprinkle on the cilantro, basil and lime zest. Cut the pizza into wedges and serve at once.

A Note from LaDonna Rose
How do you know if shrimp is cooked? There are a few different ways you can do so:
1. Look at the color of the shrimp: Fully cooked shrimp have a pink hue to them.
2. Examine the shape: When a shrimp is cooked to perfection, the tail end will start to curl upward into a C-shape.
3. Feel the texture of the shrimp: Cooked shrimp will be firm to the touch, but relatively soft. Think of al dente pasta, but in shrimp form. If shrimp is overcooked, the texture will be rubbery.

Mediterranean Shrimp

Serves **4**

1½ pounds baby **potatoes,** cut into wedges
2 large **fennel** bulbs, stalks discarded, bulbs halved lengthwise, cored and
  cut into 1-inch-thick wedges through the stem end
3 tablespoons **olive oil,** divided, plus extra for drizzling
sea **salt** and ground black **pepper**
2 pounds jumbo **shrimp,** peeled and deveined
1 cup grape or cherry **tomatoes**
2 teaspoons fresh **oregano leaves**
zest of ½ **lemon**
½ cup **feta cheese,** crumbled
½ cup **Kalamata olives,** pitted and halved
¼ cup flat leaf **parsley,** chopped

Adjust oven rack to lower middle position and heat your oven to 400°F. Toss potatoes, fennel, 2 tablespoons oil, ½ teaspoon salt and ¼ teaspoon pepper together in a bowl. Spread vegetables in a single layer on a rimmed baking sheet lined with parchment paper and roast just until tender, about 30 minutes.

Pat the shrimp dry with paper towels. Toss shrimp, tomatoes oregano, lemon zest, remaining 1 tablespoon of oil, ½ teaspoon salt and ¼ teaspoon pepper together in a bowl.

Using spatula, flip potatoes and fennel so browned sides are facing up. Scatter shrimp over top. Return sheet to oven and roast until shrimp are cooked through, 6 to 8 minutes. Sprinkle olives, feta and parsley over top and drizzle with extra oil and serve.

SHRIMP FAJITAS

Serves **4**

1½ pounds **jumbo shrimp,** peeled and deveined
¼ cup **olive oil,** divided
1 **lime**
1 medium **onion,** thinly sliced
2 **red bell peppers,** cored and thinly sliced
8 small flour **tortillas**

<u>Fajita Seasoning</u>
1½ teaspoons **chili powder**
1½ teaspoons ground **cumin**
1 teaspoon **garlic powder**
½ teaspoon **paprika**
½ teaspoon **oregano**
½ teaspoon sea **salt**
¼ teaspoon ground black **pepper**

<u>Toppings</u>
avocado (or guacamole), red cabbage, cilantro, jalapenos, sour cream and salsa

Seasoning: In a small bowl, stir together the seasoning ingredients.

Pat shrimp dry with paper towels. In a large bowl, add the shrimp, 2 tablespoons of olive oil, the juice from half a lime and the fajita seasoning. Toss it all together until the shrimp is well coated and set aside to marinate.

Heat two tablespoons of oil in a large nonstick sauté pan over medium heat. Add the onions and bell peppers and sauté for 4-5 minutes or until softened. Transfer to a plate.

In the same skillet, add the shrimp and cook for about 2-3 minutes or until they turn pink.

Add the onions and **bell peppers** back into the skillet, give everything a toss and squeeze more lime juice on top. Serve immediately with tortillas and extra toppings such as avocado, guacamole, sour cream or salsa.

SPAGHETTI SQUASH SHRIMP SCAMPI

Serves **4**

1 medium-large **spaghetti squash**
1 tablespoon **olive oil**
sea **salt** and freshly ground black **pepper**
2 tablespoons **butter**
1½ pounds large **shrimp,** peeled and deveined
2 tablespoons **butter**
1 tablespoon **garlic,** minced
1 **shallot,** minced
⅓ cup **white wine** or organic chicken broth
1 tablespoon **lemon juice**
3 cups baby **spinach,** tough stems removed
½ cup fresh **basil** leaves, sliced thin
⅛ teaspoon **red pepper flakes**
¼ cup **Parmesan cheese,** freshly grated

Preheat your oven to 400°F. With a large, sharp knife carefully cut the squash in half lengthwise. Scrape out the seeds. Brush with oil and season with salt and pepper. Place squash cut-side down in an oven-safe dish; add ¼ cup water and cover the dish with aluminum foil. Place into the oven and roast for about 45 minutes or until the flesh is tender. Remove from oven and let cool slightly. Using a fork, scrape the squash to create long strands.

Pat shrimp dry with paper towels and season with salt and pepper. Melt butter in a large nonstick sauté pan over medium-high heat. Sear the shrimp until just cooked through, 1-2 minutes per side. Remove the shrimp to a plate and set aside.

Add the garlic and shallot and cook for 1 minute. Add the wine and lemon juice, scraping up the browned bits with a wooden spoon. Add the squash and spinach to the pan. Cook, stirring occasionally, until the squash is heated through and the spinach is wilted. Stir in basil, red pepper flakes, salt and pepper to taste. Serve immediately, topped with the reserved shrimp and garnish with Parmesan.

ANGEL HAIR PASTA WITH SHRIMP

Serves **4**

8 ounces **angel hair pasta,** cook according to package directions,
   reserve 1 cup cooking water, then drain
1 tablespoon **butter**
½ cup **green onions,** sliced thin
8 cloves **garlic,** sliced thin
¼ cup dry **white wine** (or cooking wine)
1 cup **heavy whipping cream**
½ cup organic **chicken broth**
¼ cup Parmesan cheese, grated
¼ teaspoon **nutmeg**
1 teaspoon sea **salt**
½ teaspoon ground black **pepper**
1 pound **medium shrimp,** peeled and deveined
2 tablespoons fresh **chives,** sliced
Parmesan cheese for garnish

Melt butter in a 12-inch frying pan over medium heat. Add green onions and garlic. Cook, stirring often, until fragrant. Stir in white wine, cream, broth, Parmesan, nutmeg, salt and pepper. Bring to a simmer, reduce heat to medium-low and cook until cream is slightly thickened, about 3 minutes.

Add shrimp to the cream sauce, increase heat to medium and cook, stirring occasionally, just until shrimp are pink, 3-4 minutes.

Add pasta and stir to coat. Stir in reserved pasta water (mixture will appear soupy, then thicken as it stands) and toss in chives. Add more salt and pepper if you like. Garnish with Parmesan cheese.

JAMBALAYA WRAPS

Makes **2**

¾ cup **cooked white rice**
2 tablespoons **olive oil**
1 cup **kielbasa sausage,** thinly sliced on the bias
⅓ cup **onion,** diced
⅓ cup **celery,** diced
⅓ cup **green bell pepper,** diced
8 **large shrimp,** peeled and deveined
2 teaspoons **garlic,** chopped
½ cup **shredded cooked chicken**
⅓ cup **cherry tomatoes,** quartered
2 tablespoons fresh **parsley,** chopped
1 teaspoon **Tabasco sauce**
¼ teaspoon sea **salt,** or more to taste
2 burrito-size flour **tortillas** (10-inch)

In a medium sauté pan, heat the oil over medium-high heat. Add the sausage and brown, about three minutes. Stir in onion, celery and bell pepper; sauté about 5 minutes. Add the shrimp and garlic; cook, stirring constantly, until shrimp turns opaque, about 3 minutes.

Add the chicken, tomatoes and rice; cook just to heat through, about 3 minutes. Stir in parsley and Tabasco; season to taste with salt.

Divide jambalaya wraps evenly between tortillas; roll to wrap.

CREAMY SHRIMP FLORENTINE

Serves **2**

½ pound **linguine pasta,** cooked according to package directions, drain
2 tablespoons **butter**
1 tablespoon **garlic,** minced
1 pound large **shrimp,** peeled and deveined
1½ cups **heavy cream**
½ cup organic **chicken broth**
1½ teaspoons **garlic powder**
2 teaspoons **Italian seasoning**
¾ cup **Parmesan cheese,** shredded
1 cup **spinach,** chopped
8 torn **basil leaves**
½ cup jarred **sun dried tomato strips** in oil, drained
½ teaspoon sea **salt**
¼ teaspoon black **pepper**

Heat the butter in a large sauté pan over medium-high heat. Add the garlic and sauté for 1 minute.

Pat the shrimp dry with paper towels and add them to the pan. Cook for 1-2 minutes per side until just opaque and cooked through, turning them with tongs. Remove the shrimp and set aside on a plate.

Add the heavy cream, chicken broth, garlic powder, Italian seasoning and Parmesan cheese. Whisk over medium heat until it starts to thicken. Add the spinach, basil, sun dried tomatoes, salt and pepper and let it simmer until the spinach starts to wilt. Add the shrimp back to the pan, remove from the heat and serve over pasta.

SWEET TREATS

RHUBARB ANGEL DESSERT

Serves **8**

1½ cups **graham cracker crumbs**
3 tablespoons **butter,** melted
1 cup **sugar**
2 tablespoons **cornstarch**
4 cups fresh **rhubarb,** diced
1 (3-ounce) package raspberry or strawberry **gelatin**
1 (8-ounce) frozen **whipped topping,** thawed
1½ cups miniature **marshmallows**

Preheat your oven to 350°F.

In a small bowl, combine cracker crumbs and butter. Press mixture into a 7x11-inch baking dish. Bake for 10 minutes or until lightly browned. Cool on a wire rack. In a large saucepan combine the sugar, cornstarch and rhubarb. Bring to a boil; cook and stir for 2-3 minutes or until thickened and rhubarb is tender. Remove from heat; stir in gelatin until dissolved. Cover and refrigerate 1 hour.

Spoon rhubarb mixture over crust. Combine whipped topping and marshmallows; spread over rhubarb mixture. Refrigerate at least 1 hour before serving.

EASY FRUIT TART

Serves 4

1 (9½ by 9-inch) sheet **puff pastry,** thawed
2 teaspoons coarse **raw sugar**
⅛ teaspoon ground **cinnamon**
4 ounces **cream cheese,** softened
½ cup plus 2 tablespoons smooth **strawberry jelly**
1 teaspoon **vanilla** extract
3 cups **fresh berries**

Adjust your oven rack to the upper-middle position and heat your oven to 425°F. Line a baking sheet with parchment paper. Unfold the puff pastry onto the prepared baking sheet.

Brush a ½ inch border along the edges of the pastry with water. Fold the long edges of the pastry over by ½ inch, then fold the short edges over by ½ inch. Working lengthwise, lightly score the outer edge of all folded edges of the tart with a pairing knife. To prevent the center of the tart from puffing up in the oven, poke the dough repeatedly with a fork.

Combine the sugar and cinnamon and sprinkle the mixture over the inside of the tart shell. Transfer to the oven and bake until the pastry and sugar are a deep golden brown, 15 to 20 minutes. Transfer to a wire rack and let cool at least 1 hour.

While the crust is baking, stir the cream cheese, 2 tablespoons jelly and vanilla in a bowl until smooth. Spread the cream cheese mixture over the inside of the cooled tart shell. Place remaining ½ cup jelly in a large microwave-safe bowl and microwave on high power until the jelly melts, about 30 seconds. Add the berries to the bowl and toss gently until coated with jelly.

Spoon the berries over the cream cheese mixture and refrigerate until the jelly is set, at least 1 hour and up to 4 hours. Let sit at room temperature for 30 minutes. Serve.

RAINBOW FRUIT KEBABS

Serves **6**

strawberries, small oranges, pineapple, raspberries, kiwi, grapes and blueberries
12 skewers

Thread fruit onto skewers and serve.

BARBECUED BANANAS

Makes **6**
6 unpeeled ripe **bananas**
6 tablespoons **brown sugar**
6 tablespoons **orange marmalade**
ice cream or **whipped topping**

Cut a lengthwise slit in each banana, being careful not to cut all the way through; spread open slightly. Gently pack 1 tablespoon brown sugar inside each. Drizzle marmalade over the brown sugar. Grill, without lid, over medium heat 4 minutes on each side.

Top each grilled banana with a small scoop of ice cream or a dallop of whipped cream. Serve immediately.

ULTIMATE COOKIE BARS

24 bars

½ cup **butter,** melted
1½ cups **graham cracker crumbs**
1 (11-ounce) pkg. semi-sweet **chocolate chips**
1 (11-ounce) pkg. **butterscotch baking chips**
1 cup flaked **coconut**
1½ cups **pecans** or **walnuts,** chopped
1 (14-ounce) can **sweetened condensed milk**

Preheat your oven to 350°F. Spray a 9 x 13-inch baking dish with nonstick cooking spray.

In a small bowl, combine cracker crumbs and butter. Press mixture into the bottom of the baking dish. Add chocolate chips, butterscotch chips, coconut and nuts in layers to completely cover the crust. Drizzle condensed milk evenly over the top. Gently press down with a fork. Bake for 30 minutes or until beginning to brown. Remove from oven and allow to cool for 10 minutes. While still warm, loosen bars from the side of the pan to prevent them from sticking. Cut in bars. Store tightly covered.

EASY TIRAMISU

Serves **6**

4 ounces **cream cheese,** softened
1 ½ cups **cold milk**
1 (3-ounce) package **instant vanilla pudding**
2 (3-ounce) packages **lady fingers,** split (or pound cake)
⅓ cup **strong coffee,** cooled
1 (8-ounce) container frozen **whipped topping,** thawed
1 square semi-sweet **chocolate,** grated

In a large bowl, beat cream cheese with a mixer until smooth. Gradually add milk. Add pudding mix. Beat on low speed for 2 minutes. **Sprinkle cut sides of lady fingers with coffee.** Place ⅓ of the lady fingers on the bottom of an 8x8-inch baking dish; top with layers of ⅓ each of the pudding mixture and whipped topping; sprinkle with ⅓ of the grated chocolate. Repeat all layers. (Dish will be full) Refrigerate 3 hours or until ready to serve.

INDEX OF RECIPES

MAIN DISHES

SWEET TREATS

Wow! What a journey Ole & I have been on. We never thought writing four Little books would be so rewarding and fun, so first and foremost we want to thank YOU for encouraging us to be as good as we can and for buying our books. You are a major source of inspiration for us and many of you are now lifelong friends.

Best Fishes!
Ole and LaDonna Rose

Other Cookbooks by LaDonna Gundersen

Available at LaDonnaRose.com
www.facebook.com/ladonnarosecooks
www.instagram.com/ladonnarosecooks

The End

Notes

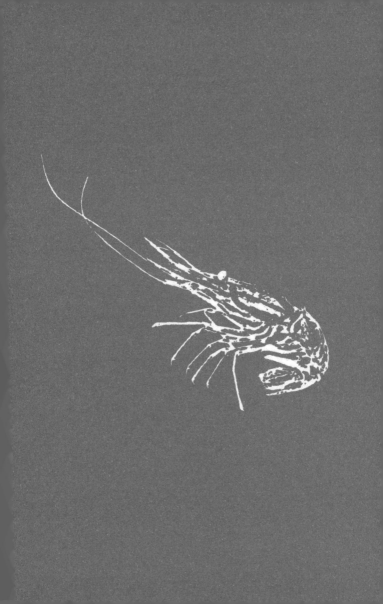